S0-CFD-891

ideals®
MOTHER'S DAY

We set aside a day each year
Which we call Mother's Day
To honor Mother, hold her close,
And cherish her in every way.

Yet wouldn't it be nice for her
If we could truly say
We set aside some time for love
To make each day our mother's day.

Minnie Klemme

ISBN 0-8249-1061-3

Publisher, Patricia A. Pingry
Editor, Peggy Schaefer
Art Director, Patrick McRae
Production Manager, Jan Johnson
Editorial Assistant, Kathleen Gilbert
Copy Editor, Joan Anderson

Front and back covers by Gerald Koser

Inside front cover by Ed Cooper

Inside back cover from FPG International

IDEALS—Vol. 45, No. 3 May MCMLXXXVIII IDEALS (ISSN 0019-137X) is published eight times a year,
February, March, May, June, August, September, November, December
by IDEALS PUBLISHING CORPORATION, Nelson Place at Elm Hill Pike, Nashville, Tenn. 37214
Second class postage paid at Nashville, Tennessee, and additional mailing offices.
Copyright©MCMLXXXVIII by IDEALS PUBLISHING CORPORATION.
POSTMASTER: Send address changes to Ideals, Post Office Box 148000, Nashville, Tenn. 37214-8000
All rights reserved. Title IDEALS registered U.S. Patent Office.

SINGLE ISSUE—$3.95
ONE-YEAR SUBSCRIPTION—eight consecutive issues as published—$17.95
TWO-YEAR SUBSCRIPTION—sixteen consecutive issues as published—$31.95
Outside U.S.A., add $6.00 per subscription year for postage and handling.

The cover and entire contents of IDEALS are fully protected by copyright and must
not be reproduced in any manner whatsoever. Printed and bound in U.S.A.

Wild Bouquet

Craig Sathoff

When sunbeams smile warmly
To greet each new May day,
It's time to roam the fresh green fields
And pick a wild bouquet.

Around the once-used windmill
That stands upon the hill,
Pink daisies bloom in bright display
And lilacs grow there still.

We'll use their pastel loveliness
To soften our bouquet,
Pick next some wild roses,
And then be on our way.

Some frilly sprigs of mustard shrub
And fragrant clover, too,
Along with thick-veined plantain leaves
Will give a sylvan hue.

The regal white of Queen Anne's Lace
Will lend the dignity,
And purple-velvet iris
Will hint of majesty.

'Twill be a splendid grouping
That makes the gay bouquet
A tribute to the welcome spring
Which beautifies our way.

Photo Opposite
BLOOMS OF JOY
M. Thonig
H. Armstrong Roberts, Inc.

Photo Overleaf
SIMPSON BOTANICAL GARDENS
SHORE ACRES STATE PARK
Bob Clemenz Photography

Coming of May

Stella Craft Tremble

The month of May wears a green skirt
And holds her lap of flowers,
Then skipping lightly on her way
Leaves warm and sunny hours.

She dresses woods and vales in green,
Throws daisies on the hill,
Then treading softly in the glade,
She dissipates the chill.

The Alder tree lets down her hair,
Reflected in the pool;
The mountain paths wear silver veils
When early morns are cool.

We've longed for Spring: now she has come
With warmth and laughter gay,
To wake the world and bless the earth
This flowery month of May!

Photo Opposite
HOUSE IN SPRING
Fred M. Dole Productions

Intrusion

Mina Morris Scott

I lifted a leaf
And there I found
A secret beauty so profound
I paused in breathless wonder.

How could such treasure
Lie concealed,
Only by chance to be revealed
With emerald roof asunder?

I stood transfixed
And gazed until
Such reverence did my being fill,
I could absorb no more.

Three tiny eggs
In gauzy nest—
I looked long on their loveliness,
Then closed the little door.

Music unborn,
With brilliant wings—
A host of precious promised things
Within that cradle lay.

No further did I
Dare intrude
Or risk offense by action crude.
Softly I stole away.

Photo Opposite
HANGING GARDENS
GLACIER NATIONAL PARK
Tom Algire
H. Armstrong Roberts, Inc.

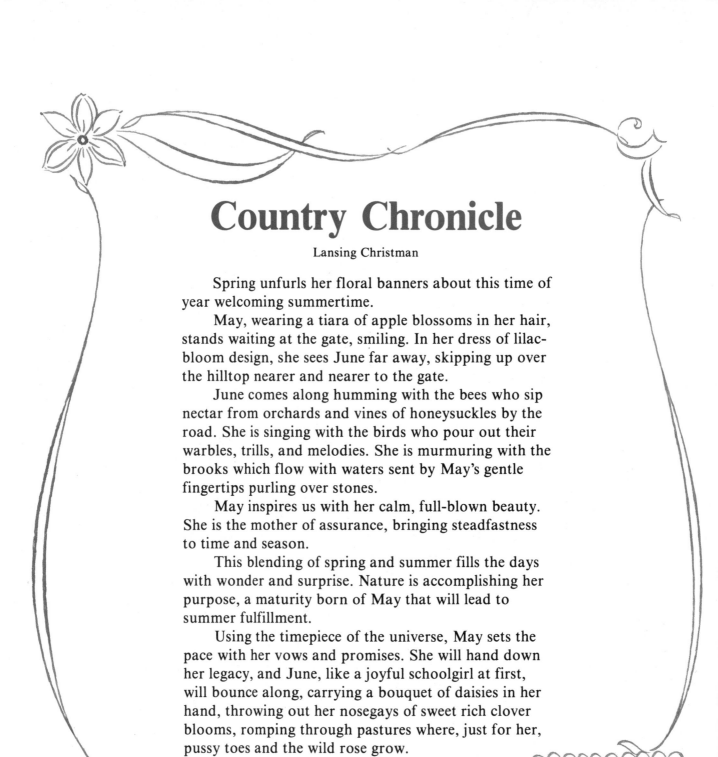

Country Chronicle

Lansing Christman

Spring unfurls her floral banners about this time of year welcoming summertime.

May, wearing a tiara of apple blossoms in her hair, stands waiting at the gate, smiling. In her dress of lilac-bloom design, she sees June far away, skipping up over the hilltop nearer and nearer to the gate.

June comes along humming with the bees who sip nectar from orchards and vines of honeysuckles by the road. She is singing with the birds who pour out their warbles, trills, and melodies. She is murmuring with the brooks which flow with waters sent by May's gentle fingertips purling over stones.

May inspires us with her calm, full-blown beauty. She is the mother of assurance, bringing steadfastness to time and season.

This blending of spring and summer fills the days with wonder and surprise. Nature is accomplishing her purpose, a maturity born of May that will lead to summer fulfillment.

Using the timepiece of the universe, May sets the pace with her vows and promises. She will hand down her legacy, and June, like a joyful schoolgirl at first, will bounce along, carrying a bouquet of daisies in her hand, throwing out her nosegays of sweet rich clover blooms, romping through pastures where, just for her, pussy toes and the wild rose grow.

Photo Opposite
SUISUN VALLEY, CALIFORNIA
Ed Cooper Photo

As We Watch

John Clarence Novack

A smile in her sleep endears to ourselves
The child that fell slowly (since quarter till twelve)
To a magical slumber in a dear little bed
Blessed by the stirring of an innocent head.

Oh, love! How can our watching tell
What day-dazzling laughter within her dwells?
And where do her sleep-filled visions go?
Only God and the angels know.

Little Overalls of Blue

Mary Drummond

In little overalls of blue
And hat of widest brim,
With rake and hoe and shovel, too,
Just big enough for him,
In midday bright spring sunshine
My laddie digs the soil
For the garden to be planted by
This little gardener's toil.

Such wondrous ways of gardening
You surely never saw.
He's planting baked potatoes 'cause
He doesn't like them raw.
Those paper roses by the fence,
He's sure they'll take a root,
And here he planted sister's doll
To grow a china foot.

He's put in popcorn, candy beans,
And one small onion set.
Tomorrow he will dig to see
If they have sprouted yet.
And by such labor, worried,
He climbs on Mother's lap;
This busy little farmer boy
Is ready for his nap.

Reflections

Seven

John J. Pepping

She has freckles and pigtails,
And a little pug nose,
And a mouth that keeps going
Like it never will close.

She can handle a skateboard
And a two-wheeler bike;
She can catch a football
And fly her own kite.

She's too tall to call little,
Yet too small to call big.
She is not quite a branch,
But she's more than a twig.

Like all little girls
She is cute and she's coy;
But as most girls of seven
She's a little tomboy.

But her eyes have a softness
And a twinkling glow;
She gets into your heart
And you can't let her go.

Editor's Note: Readers are invited to submit unpublished, original poetry, short anecdotes, and humorous reflections on life for possible publication in future *Ideals* issues. Please send copies only; manuscripts will not be returned. Writers will receive $10 for each published submission. Send materials to "Readers' Reflections," Ideals Publishing Corporation, Nelson Place at Elm Hill Pike, Nashville, Tennessee 37214.

Portrait of a Boy

Pearl Bloch Segall

Small fingers reach
To intertwine
Around a willow branch;
No sturdy hand
Supports him, yet
He's willing to take this chance.

A small boy's trusting,
Testing grip
On slim and verdant bough;
He does not think
Of anything
Except this challenge now.

Oh, for those years
That swiftly passed
Like birds at lightning speed . . .
But willow boughs
And small, lean boys
Still live in time and deed.

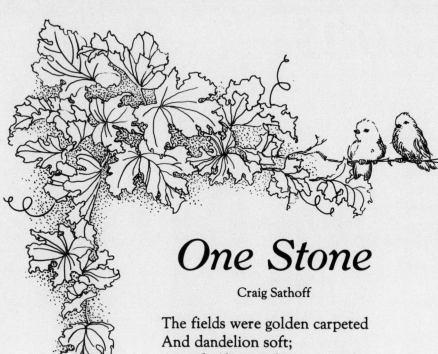

One Stone

Craig Sathoff

The fields were golden carpeted
And dandelion soft;
A cardinal treated me to song
As he flew by aloft.

And then I stopped my springtime walk,
For standing all alone,
I chanced upon a glimmering
And very lovely stone.

It rested firmly in the ground
And raised its smiling face
As if to hold its beauty back
By giving just a trace.

Each spring I love the daffodils,
I love the robin's song;
I search the timber every day
Till mushrooms come along.

But oh, how unexpected was
The beauty of that stone,
Sparkling in the springtime sun
Where it stood all alone!

Photo Opposite
CHRISTMAS COVE, MAINE
Fred Sieb

To My Son

Ruth Rodier Taylor

I could wish that I were wise,
To keep the innocence in your eyes,
To shield you from the truths that pain,
To show but rainbows in the rain.

I could wish that I were strong,
To clear your path of every wrong,
Never let you shed a tear,
Or know the terror of a fear.

Would life be heaven, then, for you,
If these my wishes could come true?

I am not wise, and yet I know
That wishing doesn't make it so;
And joys are never quite so sweet
As after problems that we meet.

What pride the prize that you have won
If there was not a race to run?

Photo Opposite
MOTHER'S LOVE
Mark J. Barrett
H. Armstrong Roberts, Inc.

Country Morning

Judy Sizemore

"Come on, Mommy!"

My daughter grabs her lunch box and dashes out the door. I wrap a scarf around my neck and follow her. What a shock it is to leave the cozy warmth of our living room, the crackling fire, the cheery lights, and plunge into this world of darkness and cold! I shine the flashlight on the porch thermometer as we hurry past. Two below this morning.

"How do you stand it?" friends ask when I tell them how early Robin and I get up, how far we walk to meet her school bus. "It must be awful."

Awful? I'll admit there is an occasional morning when the weather is bad or one of us doesn't feel well and I fire up the old truck and drive out. But most mornings are like this one; we don't want to shatter the pre-dawn silence with the roar of a motor. Our walk down the dark road together is a magical, sharing time, the best fifteen minutes of the day.

"Look, Mommy, the world's all covered with diamonds," Robin exclaims gleefully, playing her flashlight across the hard sparkle of frost.

And so it is. It's a beautiful world out here, and it's all ours. We can sing without worrying if our voices are off-key. There's no one to hear us but the stars. Even the chickens are still asleep.

"Yesterday we studied all about the sun," Robin tells me. "Did you know it's our closest star?"

It's a strange thing. When she comes home in the afternoon and I ask her what she did at school, her answer is invariably, "Nothing much." But now, in the crisp clarity of early morning, it all comes tumbling out: what she learned, who sat next to her in the lunchroom, who was sent into the hall for whispering.

The blackness is thinning to gray when we come to the spot where our driveway crosses a creek. We stop for a moment to listen.

"Why do puddles freeze before the creek?" Robin asks as we resume our walk.

Later in the day I might be too busy to answer her, but now I have time.

"I like puddles," she announces. "I like to crunch up the ice with my boots."

I like it, too.

"You know what I'm going to do when I grow up?" she asks, skipping ahead. "I'm going to live on a farm and raise horses, and be an artist, and in the evenings I'm going to give dance lessons."

"When I grow up . . . " So many of her sentences start with that phrase now. I look at her in the pale light. It won't be long. A dozen years and she'll be off to college . . . or wherever her dreams take her.

That's why these walks are so precious to me. That's why I'm glad we live way down a country lane and have to walk a quarter mile to the bus stop. She won't always be my little girl, but I'll always have the memory of these quiet, dark mornings, of our special time together. And I hope she'll carry the memory with her wherever she goes. I hope it will be a memory she can rest her head on when she's tired, draw strength from when she's weary, find peace in when she's troubled.

"There's the bus!" she cries, and we sprint the last hundred yards, making it just in time for a quick hug before the bus swallows her up and takes her away.

The sun's peeking over the horizon as I head back up the drive. I think about her on the bus, laughing and chatting with her friends. I think about my own busy day ahead: the livestock to feed, the house to clean, the shed roof that needs to be repaired.

I'm ready for it now. I face my day with a smile, filled up with the magic I found walking with my daughter in the darkness and cold of a country morning.

A Child You Love

Garnett Ann Schultz

Being with a child you love
Is like a day in spring,
With cotton clouds all fleecy white
And songs your heart can sing.

It's magic in a special way
To have this child about;
Seeing life through newer eyes
Brings joy without a doubt.

Sharing in a sweet child's dream
With its fantastic charms,
Holding close a little one
Within your loving arms,

Feeling fresh as summer rain,
As pure as winter's snow—
These open up life's wonder
And like the flowers, you grow.

Being with a child you love
Puts music in the air;
A little face so soft and dear
Brings gladness everywhere.

You find yourself and this child stuck
Like bubblegum on shoe,
Knowing that this child you love
Has love untold for you.

BUBBLING OVER
Norman/Zefa
H. Armstrong Roberts, Inc.

Being with a child you love
Makes life so much worthwhile,
Sharing happy hours of play,
Delightful, wondrous smiles.

And sometimes when you pause to think,
You thank God in a prayer
That he has sent this child to love
And placed him in your care.

Mother's Little Helper

Mrs. Paul E. King

I stand upon my little stool
As happy as can be,
With Mommy's apron 'round my waist
(It's dreadfully long for me).
Oh, what fun to help wash dishes
As bubbles to the ceiling fly!
I feel quite grown and wonderful
Helping Mother make a pie!

I help to roll the cookie dough
And eat a bite or two
Then cut it out in animals—
Enough to fill a zoo.
I feel moisture on my forehead
And dampness in my curl;
But I don't mind it one small bit
'Cause I'm Mother's helper girl!

My Favorite Recipes

Phyllis Michael

I have some favorite recipes,
Dear little daughter of mine;
My mother gave them all to me
And I'll pass them down the line:
There's her chili sauce and her cherry pie,
Her crisp ginger cookies, too,
And her special kind of dark fruit cake—
Well, just to name a few.

Then right at the top of the very first page
In Mother's own writing it reads:
"Just add with the other ingredients here
All the love that everyone needs;
Mix well with good humor, enough for each day,
Add a prayer of thanksgiving and bake
In the oven of time so it turns out all right.
What a wonderful feast it will make!"

A Thousand Million Questions

Phyllis Michael

There's a thousand million questions
That my daughter wants to know—
In the middle of the summer
When it's hot, why can't it snow?
How can little bitty brown seeds
Into red tomatoes grow?
How do dark clouds up above us
Bring the rain just like they do?
Why does grass grow all around us
'Stead of just a blade or two?
Why do puppies bark to wake us
While Sue's kittens only mew?

There's a thousand million questions
That my daughter wants to ask.
Is it, then, dear Lord, too brazen
Since to answer is my task,
That I beg, oh, please don't let me
Wear a grim forbidding mask;
Let me spare a workday moment
To learn more about such things,
Give me wisdom, daily wisdom,
From your secret hidden springs—
There's a thousand million questions
That my darling daughter brings.

A Soul Is Born

Haven Hubbard

How can we say, how can we sing
    Of new life born with vibrant cry,
    A signal to a listening sky
A newborn soul is on the wing!

A presence filling all the room,
    A ray of light that shines on earth,
    Another spirit comes to birth,
A flower suddenly in bloom.

And when he learns to move and crawl,
    Oh, give this small explorer space
    To see the world at his own pace.
Discovery is all in all.

Erect no barrier to his mind;
    Allow his feet and brain to run.
    For he will learn while having fun,
And if he seeks, then he will find.

An Eloquent Smile

Andrew Daughters

I saw a mother lean one day
Above the crib where baby lay.
And as the mother cooed and spoke,
The smile upon her face that broke
Was eloquent with love and pride
That could not be restrained inside.

The child who lay was very small.
Her tongue, her mouth, her voice were all
Experimental still and new.
Her eyes just learned to focus, too.

And then, between the pair there passed
A sharing, not to be surpassed,
As on the infant's face there came
A smile that flickered like a flame.
The smile that passed from face to face
Brought heaven's own radiance to the place.

I wondered, seeing what transpired,
What magic had that act inspired.
I wondered how the baby knew
What muscles bring a smile to view.
And how did baby ever guess
A smile so mirrors happiness?

What joy to see the spectacle
Of sharing, life's first miracle.
For on the day that smile was worn,
Communication new was born.

Poetry of Life

Garnett Ann Schultz

O little child with shining eyes
And tender heart that laughs and cries,
Enthusiasms all your own,
In meadows bright you pause and roam.

O little child, accepting all
The summer morn when redbirds call,
Your world a new adventure place
Where sunbeams catch a smiling face,

Resplendent in life's simple things,
A miracle that loving brings,
Believing heart, a faith divine—
So much beauty you've made mine.

O little child, who seeks the skies
And thrills to lilting lullabies
You hold no hurt, you know no strife,
A child—the poetry of life.

Once a Mother, Always a Mother

Pamela Kennedy

I sat with my father beside the bed where his mother lay, like a fragile rose in pink satin and eyelet. Her white hair framed her face like a wispy cloud and her bright blue eyes sparkled. Full, plump pillows braced her back and her hands gestured grandly as she talked. Ninety years hadn't dulled her voice as she spoke of old friends and recent events with equal interest. My father glanced at his watch surreptitiously, he thought, but Grandma caught it.

"Time to go, is it?" she said, then a sigh escaped. "You really shouldn't rush about so, you know. It isn't good for you. Bad for your nerves, makes them all jangly. Remember how you used to get in school when you'd get too many irons in the fire?"

Father nodded, smiling a bit.

"Well, same thing now, only now you're too big for me to send to bed early!" She pointed her finger at him and shook her head in mock anger.

"I know, Mama," my father responded, taking the accusing hand in his. "I'm fine. Don't you worry."

"Once a mother, always a mother," Grandma stated with finality.

My father laughed and agreed, kissing her cheek. "See you tomorrow, Mama."

"I should hope so!" she countered, waving us off like two pesky, but well-loved children.

Thirty years have passed since that afternoon, but Grandma's words still rattle around in my head: "Once a mother, always a mother."

Is it true? Is there something about mothering that stays with you for life, perhaps leaving you with mothering antibodies of some sort?

At first I doubted it. But that was, of course, before I was a mother. That's when I found out that having a mother and being one are two entirely different things.

Little bundles in pink and blue blankets weld themselves to your arms and before you know it, they've wormed their way into your heart. There's no denying it. Once you've loved your own child, an interesting process begins. Trees and clouds, rain and sun, streets and bridges, dogs and cats all become sources of fresh fascination—and concern. Courageous women see dangers lurking in the most unlikely places. What if the vase falls? What if the door slams? What if the baby trips?

As the little darlings grow, the inevitable "Mother liturgy" begins: "Don't forget your coat." "Do you have a handkerchief?" "What about your lunch?" "Where will you be after school?" "Are you sure he's a nice boy?"

It doesn't matter how old the child is. The mother feelings never stop. You see the young man and remember the boy on his new bike for the first time. The young bride brings back memories of a pig-tailed girl playing dress-up or crying over a broken date. It's hard to let these moments pass and not offer just a bit of mother advice: "Now remember to put your best foot forward." "Please, dear, don't twist your hair like that." "Still biting those nails?" "Come on now, just look on the bright side!" It's as if the mother in us refuses to stop functioning. Tuned to perfection during eighteen or twenty years, this part of us somehow switches into automatic and just keeps going even after the child is grown.

It was windy today and the apples were plump and ripe on the tree in the backyard. My daughter called and asked if she and Emily could come over to pick some fruit. They arrived in a burst of energy and noise as Emily bounded in the front door calling, "Gramma, we're going to make applesauce for Daddy! Mama says you have an applesauce tree!"

Laughing, we gathered a pail and ladder

from the garage and headed for the tree, eager to hunt for "applesauces."

"Don't you think Emily should have a jacket, dear?" I asked.

My daughter looked exasperated and shook her head. "It's nice out today, Mom; she's fine."

I recognized the look. I'd given it often enough to my own mother. Buttoning my sweater, I followed my granddaughter to the "applesauce tree," hurrying to steady the ladder for her. Suddenly I could see Grandma winking through the fluttering leaves, her blue eyes smiling and in the autumn breeze I think I could hear her saying, "Once a mother, always a mother!"

Just Like Mine

Phyllis Michael

I want my home to be like the home
    I knew when I was small—
A home where faith was all around,
    Where love grew on each wall.
I want my child to know the peace
    I know today because
My mother took the time to pray,
    To teach me God's own laws.
I want to keep my kitchen bright,
    My table set with grace,
The kind it takes to make my child
    Feel welcome in this place.

I want to play, to take time out
    To hear each childish word—
To talk to him, to walk with him,
    To let him know he's heard.
I want to make him feel each day
    This home is his home, too—
A place where we can share each joy,
    Each problem old or new.
I want to be there when he calls
    And yet not make him lean;
I want to watch him grow each day
    Strong, and true, and clean.

I could not ask for greater wealth
    Or greater gift to give
Than just a home like my home was
    Where this, my child, may live.

Mama's Homemade Bread

Angie Monnens

The sun was up, her day began,
  She bustled to and fro,
In frantic search to find the pan
  In which to mix the dough.

When utensils all were ready,
  She placed upon her head
A plain, white cap with 'lastic band
  Before she mixed the bread.

Her hair was neatly tucked inside;
  The apron tied real tight.
She set the water on the stove—
  It had to be just right.

She mixed the water with the yeast,
  Then let it set a while,
"Tonight we're going to have a feast,"
  Said Mama with a smile.

Adding salt and sifting flour,
  She started to knead the dough.
Then she let it rise an hour
  And turned the oven low.

When the dough began to rise,
   We marveled at the sight;
For soon the mass was twice its size,
   All squiggly, soft, and white.

She punched it down and shaped it
   Into loaves—some big, some small.
We kids could hardly wait until
   We'd hear our mama call:

"The bread is baked so come and eat,"
   That is all she had to say.
That golden treat made supper great,
   The end of Mama's day.

Later we put on our nightgowns
   While Mama put up her feet.
We kissed and hugged her tight and asked,
   "Is there something we can eat?"

"What did you have in mind, my dears?"
   That's what she always said,
Of course, she knew we waited for
   Another slice of bread.

Photo Overleaf
SULLIVAN HOUSE
PRESCOTT, ARIZONA
Bob Clemenz Photography

To Mother

Josephine Wiley Courtney

Memory uses golden threads
To weave her magic spell.
And deep within the cloth of life,
My heart remembers well

Each precious moment spent with you,
The laughter and the tears,
The sunshine and the shadows, too,
The storm clouds and the fears.

What matter if the thread is broken?
It's brightness will remain
To guide me through the darkness till
The sun shines once again.

A Precious Name

Loise Pinkerton Fritz

I heard them call her "Mama,"
An ordinary name.
It holds no tinge of glamour,
Nor does it speak of fame.
It's just a simple home word,
But, oh, it reaches far,
Extending to the very depths
Of children's trusting hearts.

Two syllables of loving
Is what it means to me;
Two syllables of praying
On tired, bended knees.
Two syllables of wisdom
Stored deep within her heart;
Two syllables of singing still
When all the world seems dark.

I heard them call her "Mama,"
Oh, what a sweet refrain.
It is the soothing ointment
That heals each childhood pain.
What if it holds no glamour
Nor overtures of fame?
For every woman called "Mama," yes,
It's such a precious name.

My Heart's Garden

Ruth B. Field

In my heart's garden, flowers grow,
Which brighten summer days
Like little tapers all aglow
Shining 'cross life's way;
And sweetest of the blossoms there,
A gift from God above,
Dear Mother, fairest and most rare,
You shine the light of love.

A rose and quaint forget-me-nots
Are tokens that I bring
In gratitude for all you've done
To make my own heart sing.
But I could never put in rhyme
The words that tell the maze
Of golden memories in my heart—
The love I'll have for you always.

Wash Day

Bonnie Bell Hutchison

In a little boy's pockets I happened to find
These treasures spilling forth:
A smooth, cool rock from a secret pool,
A feather from a bird flying north,
A slingshot Dad had helped to make,
A bug in a jar proudly snared
With bits of green leaves, twigs and dirt
"To hide in 'case he's scared,"
A nail bent with a hammer borrowed
From Dad's prized tool chest,
A speckled egg and two agates,
An abandoned, lopsided bird's nest.

In a little girl's pockets I happened to find
These treasures to add to the rest:
A blue hair ribbon lost jumping rope,
A doll's first homemade dress,
A piece of green glass that held the sun
In a morning game of hopscotch,
A painted hankie of bright butterflies,
And Mama's gold satin swatch,
A tiny doll, "Her name is Suzy
And she lives in a walnut shell."
A little round ball, but only two jacks,
A cup and saucer bluebell.

These things I found on wash day,
With a smile, a sigh, and a tear,
For no treasures on earth mean more to me
Than the treasures my children hold dear.

The Worth of a Neighbor

Loise Pinkerton Fritz

How great is the worth of a neighbor,
One who is trustworthy, kind,
A neighbor with whom you can visit
And share what is on your mind.
Perhaps it's an upcoming wedding
Of one who is very dear,
Or maybe the birth of a baby
That brings to your heart special cheer.

Oh, great is the worth of a neighbor
With whom we can share every thought,
With whom in the cool of the evening
We can leisurely walk and talk.
A neighbor who'll take time to listen
To all of our burdens and cares—
Oh, great is the worth of that neighbor
Who in glad times or sad times is there.

The bookplate functions as a name label, identifying the ownership of a single volume or a multi-volume library. It may be as small as a postage stamp or so large that it would properly fit only in a "coffee table" book. Beyond mere function, however, the bookplate frequently is a work of art in miniature.

The bookplate, or *ex libris* (meaning, from the books of), has a long history. Clay tablets dating before Christ included identifying marks of the owner. Later, monks and scribes who carefully copied texts by hand would include an ex libris inscription in each volume proclaiming the name of the nobleman or church library for which the book was made.

With the invention of movable type, books became available in greater numbers, and the bookplate as we know it today, a label on the inside book cover, came into being. Frequently it was a coat of arms, the same as impressed on the lord's silver serving pieces, painted on his carriage, and gold-stamped on the outside cover of his book.

The bookplate next became a woodcut which was printed and moved inside the book. As printing techniques improved, bookplates were engraved on wood and metal or etched. Earlier-age artists such as Albert Durer, Lucas Cranach, and William Hogarth designed woodcuts either specifically for bookplates or as prints which were adapted for bookplates. In colonial America, Paul Revere designed several bookplates, though he is better known as a patriot than as an engraver. Henry Dawkins, another early American, engraved several bookplates and less successfully counterfeited Continental currency. As more books were printed, they became less costly, and ordinary people owned them. They, too, wanted to show pride of ownership with a personal bookplate. These were less often armorial (coat of arms) and more likely pictorial in nature.

Knowledge of bookplates has been helpful to scholars who study heraldry, genealogy, biography, art, graphic arts, printing, and art history, and to antiquarian booksellers who may trace books to their origin through the ex libris. Since the nineteenth century there have been bookplate collecting societies, and usually such societies print information which furthers interest and scholarship in the field.

Most collectors belong to one or more bookplate societies and exchange bookplates by correspondence with other members. The etiquette of exchange is to send two prints of your personal bookplate which gives recipients one print for their own collection and a print to use for exchange. A collector's personal bookplate should not be a stock or universal bookplate on which you would write your name, but an individually designed ex libris. This may be made by a woodcut, wood or metal engraving, etching, silkscreen, printed letterpress or offset, linoleum cut, calligraphy, or another technique.

In addition to exchanging with members of ex libris societies, you may look for prints in books at used-book stores, thrift shops, swap meets, and yard sales. The sale catalogues of booksellers sometimes list the ex libris by a famous artist or for a noteworthy person, and as such demand a substantial price.

Collectors tend to specialize in plates of a particular country, century, artist, or subject (i.e., globes and maps, calligraphic plates, famous people, and legal plates).

Those who design bookplates, who write about them, and who collect them are individuals, libraries, museums, and universities. Bookplates have an international appeal. Most ex libris societies have members from the U.S., Europe, Great Britain, Canada, Japan, Australia, New Zealand, and possibly China, the latest known country to have a bookplate society. Exchange requests are often printed in several languages, and the bookplate as visual art can be enjoyed regardless of language.

For the person who enjoys adventure and history and is willing to correspond, collecting bookplates brings expanded knowledge, new friends, and time happily spent with book lovers of the past and the many artists who designed their bookplates.

Audrey Spencer Arellanes

Photos from the collection of Audrey Arellanes

Always There

Joy Belle Burgess

Home was all the tender scenes,
The little things that meant so much
And blossomed into loveliness
With Mother's warm and gentle touch.

From ruffled curtains at the sill,
The sunlight glinting through
Wove golden patterns (on the wall
And braided rug) of every hue;

The kitchen table in the nook,
A bright and sunny place
Where lilac clusters pale and sweet
Overflowed her favorite vase;

The cookies baking in the range,
The aroma that bid me come
And wait beside the oven door
In hopes that I might sample some;

Two little treasures tucked away
Upon a corner shelf,
In beauty matched with china cups,
A rosebud vase and smiling elf.

Home was all the tender scenes
That glowed with Mother's care,
But most of all I called it "home"
Because her love was always there!

My Mother's Child

Blanche Landers

I am the picture she never painted,
The book she never wrote;
I am the symphony in her soul and
The song within her throat.

I am the statue she never started,
The solitude she sought;
I am the poem she might have written—
These things to her meant naught.

I am the pain she often suffered,
The poverty life dealt;
I am the prayer she ever uttered
To heal the hurts I felt.

I am my mother's child forever
Because, from heaven above,
Her heart and hand still guide me with
Her undying love.

Staffordshire Blue

Ruth B. Field

Willow-blue Staffordshire quaint in design
On a lovely old pitcher that catches the eye,
With blue leaves and ferns in artistic fine lines,
Demure little maids play beneath a blue sky.

Linked to this favorite, the cozy room wears
Echoes of blue with touches of gold:
The luster of old wood and blue cushioned chairs,
The present enhanced with the beauty of old.

Copper and brass, a bright braided rug,
Stencils and coin spoons, an old steeple clock;
Geraniums bloom in a blue earthen mug,
A ship's lamp, some trivets, a chair that will rock.

Staffordshire blue has a rare special charm...
It brightens the room like a bright blue May sky,
And here in this room that heals like a balm,
I'll sit and I'll dream, then I'll leave by and by.

Photo Opposite
CHINA OF OLD
Vision Impact

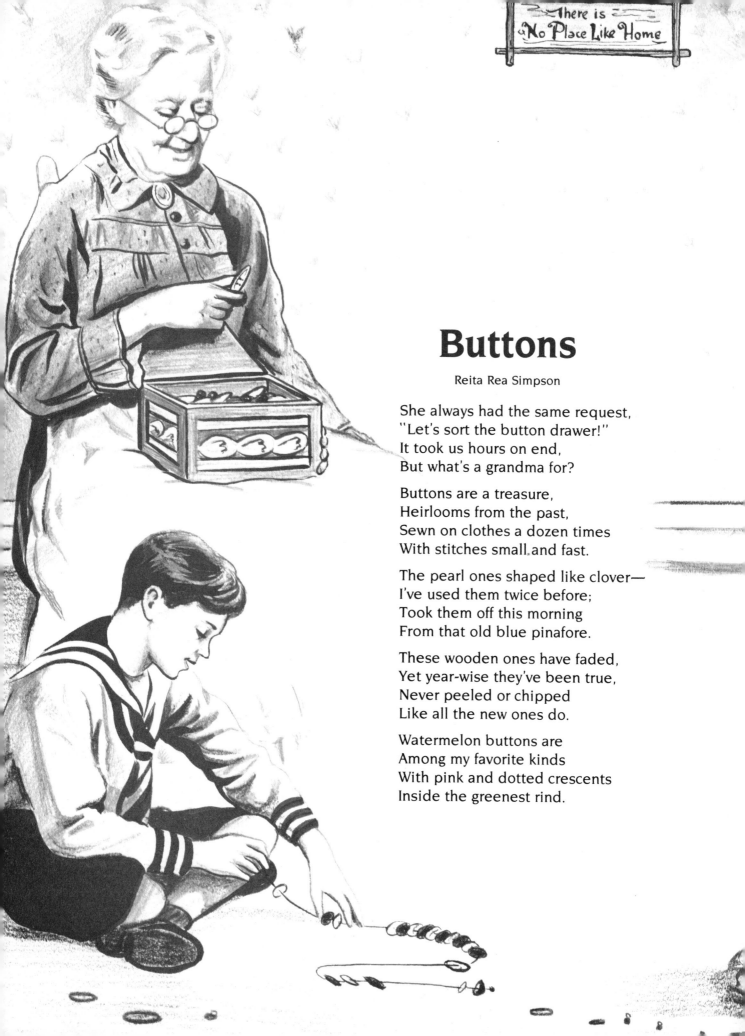

Buttons

Reita Rea Simpson

She always had the same request,
"Let's sort the button drawer!"
It took us hours on end,
But what's a grandma for?

Buttons are a treasure,
Heirlooms from the past,
Sewn on clothes a dozen times
With stitches small and fast.

The pearl ones shaped like clover—
I've used them twice before;
Took them off this morning
From that old blue pinafore.

These wooden ones have faded,
Yet year-wise they've been true,
Never peeled or chipped
Like all the new ones do.

Watermelon buttons are
Among my favorite kinds
With pink and dotted crescents
Inside the greenest rind.

Multicolored buttons,
Like flowers at the fair,
Buttoned up a Sunday coat
Your mother used to wear.

Here are all the metal ones
We'll seal away and leave
Until we have a jacket
Or a military sleeve.

These tiny baby buttons
Are from your baby dress.
Now then, this pair of ducks
Went through the wringer press!

See these black-eyed Susans?
Their backs will come apart.
Makes them nice for washin';
That's my favorite part.

She looked at all the buttons;
Which ones would she choose?—
The tiny cup-shaped crystals
With the bluest hues!

I knew she was excited,
I could see it in her eyes,
'Cause her Mama chose those buttons
When she was just her size.

A Treasured Gift

Lee Duncan Gray

My grandma made a lovely quilt
    Especially for me.
She put the squares together placing
    Stitches expertly.
She called the cloth that she had used
    "Just scraps of everything,"
But as they took on form she called
    The pattern "Wedding Ring."

I took her gift of love and skill,
    A treasure I could see,
And stored it in the cedar chest
    My true love gave to me.
Then, when the marriage vows were made,
    I placed it on the bed,
So I would be reminded of
    The words my grandma said.

"Remember child," she told me strong
    "This quilt I do bequeath
And hope you understand the message
    Woven underneath.
The cloth will wear away with age;
    A wedding ring goes on.
Your love will bring you happiness
    Long after things are gone."

Photo Opposite
WEDDING RING QUILT
Ina Mackey

Appliqué Rose Pillows

Darlene Kronschnabel

Roses, roses, everywhere! Country gardens are filled with roses of all colors and sizes from early summer to late fall. Fragrant roses were the favorite flowers in early American gardens, too. Perhaps that is why Colonial homemakers adopted the decorative flower as the central motif in their needlework and quilts.

The ever-popular "Rose of Sharon" is considered a quilting classic. Some claim a biblical source from the Song of Solomon for this delightful pattern. Early quilters copied the flowering tree-like rose in traditional patterns using pink, white, and green calico with yellow rose centers. To quiltmakers this design, with many variations, became symbolic of constant and enduring love.

There are other rose patterns, too. Ones with wreaths, leaves, and sometimes just a single large rose. There were bright red roses and dainty yellow ones growing in country gardens and they, too, were transferred into colorful appliqué patterns.

Appliqué rose blocks were designed for quilts, but they also make charming pillows. Each can be created in an almost endless variety of color and arrangement with your individual touch. The machine appliquéing makes these pillows quick and fun to make. Following are directions for making the rose pillows pictured on the front cover.

Materials Needed
(for each pillow)

Knife-edge pillow form, shredded foam for stuffing, or inner pillow*. Sturdy material for pillow front and back, plus scraps of non-fraying fabric for flowers, buds, stems, and leaves of the same general type of fabric. Select fabric of the same weight.
(Yardage given based on a 45-inch fabric)
Matching or contrasting thread, as desired
Ruler
Scissors
Straight pins
White or brown wrapping paper to make pattern

*Filling: To make your own inner pillow: Finish the appliquéd pillow cover. Turn inside out and measure carefully. Then sew an inside pillow ½ inch smaller than the decorative cover. Use unbleached muslin to give a firm, yet soft body to the completed pillow. Fill this inner form with poly-fiber filling. Stuff the muslin pillow into the appliquéd casing and carefully slip-stitch the opening.

General Directions

Using a large sheet of white or brown wrapping paper, rule off 1-inch squares. Make sure you rule off as many squares as the diagram shows. Then enlarge pattern by drawing in the same lines as in the corresponding square of the diagram. Cut out pattern pieces. Transfer individual pattern pieces to either fine sandpaper or heavy cardboard. Cut out each pattern piece exactly for a perfect fit.

Place your pattern pieces on wrong side of fabric. Carefully trace around each piece with a soft lead pencil. Cut out material.

Working with the front, determine center by first pressing flat, fold in half, then in quarters. Press. Following creases, position all flowers, buds, leaves and stems in place, overlapping each piece slightly.

Secure flower pieces by pins or fusible webbing. Zigzag around edges with close satin stitch with matching or contrasting thread.

Assembling Pillows

With right sides together and edges even, pin finished pillow front to back. Leaving ½-inch seam allowance, sew around edges, leaving an opening large enough to insert a pillow form. Carefully clip corners and turn right side out. After turning, be sure to push all corners out. A knitting needle works fine to help bring out sharp corners. Insert inner pillow form or stuffing. Slip-stitch opening. Fluff, and your pillow is ready to use.

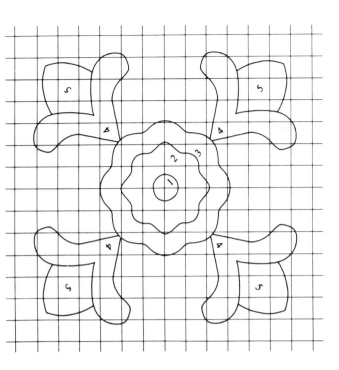

Pattern A: Two pieces of plain material 14½ inches square for front and back, about ⅛ yard each dark green, yellow, and small print material. Follow general directions.

Pattern B: Two pieces plain material 14½ inches square for front and back, ⅛ yard green for leaves, two shades of pink fabric, ⅛ yard each, to make four flowers and centers. Follow general directions.

Note: Each square equals ¼".

Pattern C: Two pieces plain material 18½ inches square for front and back, about ⅛ yard green print for leaves, ⅛ yard each of pink print and pink solid for flowers, a small yellow scrap for center, and about 25 inches of matching green bias tape for stems. Follow general directions.

Old and Dear Things

Carice Williams

The old and dear familiar things
To me are always best;
That's why I treasure old-time friends
Far more than all the rest.

Old books by old-time authors
I read and read again,
And gain a deeper knowledge of
The world because of them.

Old attics with their memories
From days of long ago,
And fine old houses with large rooms
Where cozy fires glow—

All these are dear familiar things
That soon become a part
Of all the things I carefully store
To treasure in my heart.

Prayer of Parents

Author Unknown

Great Parent of mankind,
Help me in my divine task of parenthood;

Help me to see my children's problems through their eyes;

Keep ever before me my own childhood
so that I will not expect too much.

Give me the patience of the silent stars;

Give me a sense of humor;

Help me to win them through love
instead of compelling them through fear;

Help me to teach them to see straight
and to play the game according to the rules;

Help me to teach them that every home is an altar
and that every wish is a prayer;

Help me to live my own life above doubt and skepticism;

Help me to radiate faith in the basic goodness of life;

Help me to keep the ideals of youth aglow in my own life.

Give me the strong hand for guidance
when youth falters and would turn back;

Help me to teach them to live bravely
and to meet defeat courageously;

Help me to teach them that a man's real character is
what he is when he is alone with himself in the dark;

Help me to teach them that the value of their lives
will be measured by the service they give;

Help me to teach them that true happiness is found,
not in things, but in the unfolding of their minds
and their souls;

Help me to make my life go on in theirs,
bigger, finer, nobler, than I ever dared to be.

Mending

Norma Sworski

Nimble fingers patching, mending,
Marking trails in careful line,
Steps retracing,
Interlacing
In a most unique design.

Ever moving lonely traveler
At a free and easy pace,
Seaming ridges,
Weaving bridges
Over paths of denim or lace.

In our lives the pattern changes,
Past mistakes we can erase,
By our sorrow
Each tomorrow
With more kindness we can grace.

Pressing onward, as the stitches,
With resolve each wrong to right,
Makes our patches
Glow as matches,
Blazing proof of love and light.

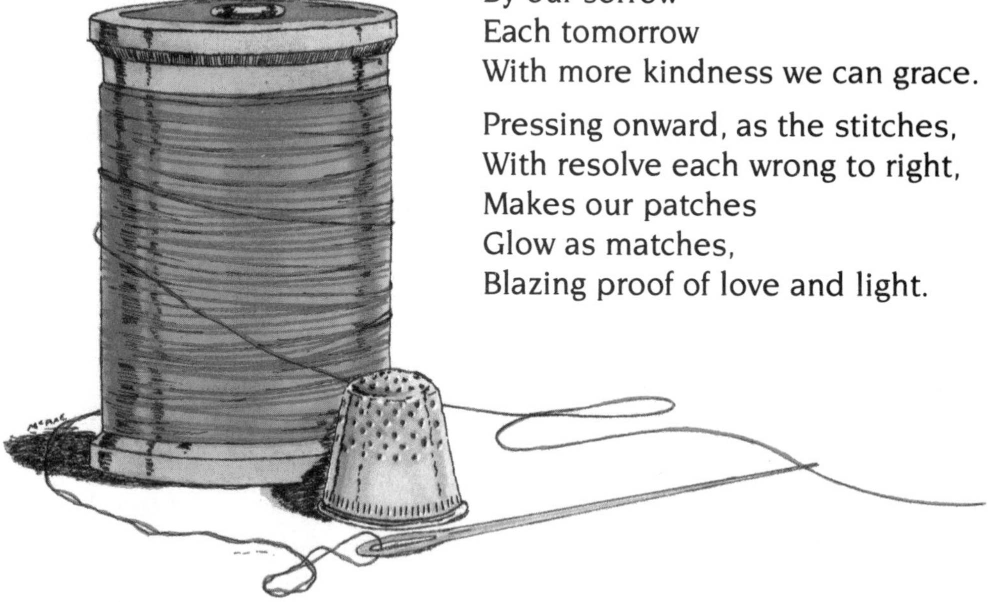

Photo Opposite
SCRAPS OF LOVE
Ina Mackey

Grandma's House

Winnifred Elsaesser

There's a house upon a hillside,
Seems it's stood for centuries there;
There's a footpath to the doorway
And a garden kept with care.

There's a kitchen filled with living
And sweet-smelling things there are,
Like apple pies a-baking
And a great big cookie jar.

Seems the kettle's always singing
And the place is bright and warm—
Gives the feeling of contentment
Like a shelter from the storm.

There's a chair that creaks when rocking
And a big cat fast asleep;
There's a grandfather clock a-ticking
And a knitting basket heap.

There's a dear sweet lady waiting,
For you see this is her house;
Yes, I'll always find a welcome
When I visit Grandma's house.

Kindness at Its Best

June Masters Bacher

Her parlor I recall was small,
And furnished sparse indeed.
It had no special style at all
But recognized a need.

I often wonder what it was
That charmed her neighbors so;
There seemed to be a secret code
That only houses know.

Or was it she who lived inside
And offered warmth and rest?
I only know Grandmother's home
Was kindness at its best.

Her parlor I recall was small,
And yet it seemed to say,
"Come in! Let's praise in simple ways
The One who made this day."

Mother's Day Menu

Carrot Quiche

Makes 6 servings

2 cups finely shredded carrots
6 eggs
1¼ cups milk
1 tablespoon instant minced onion
½ teaspoon salt
¼ teaspoon ground ginger
Dash black pepper
1½ cups shredded Cheddar cheese

Preheat oven to 350°. Bring 1 inch of water to a boil in a medium saucepan. Add carrots; cover and cook until tender, about 5 minutes. Drain thoroughly, pressing out water. Combine eggs, milk, onion, salt, ginger, and pepper in a bowl. Mix until well blended. Combine carrots and cheese in buttered 9-inch quiche dish, stirring to mix. Pour milk mixture over carrots and cheese. Set dish in a large baking pan. Pour very hot water into a baking pan to within ½ inch of top of dish. Bake for 30 to 35 minutes or until knife inserted in center comes out clean. Let stand 5 minutes before serving.

Summer Breeze

Makes 6 servings

1 teaspoon ground ginger
2½ cups whipped topping
2 small cantaloupes
1 pint strawberries
¼ cup flaked or shredded coconut, optional

Stir ginger into 1 tablespoon of the whipped topping; blend into remaining topping. Refrigerate at least 30 minutes to develop flavor. Cut cantaloupe in half crosswise or into 3 pieces lengthwise; remove seeds; reserve shells. Carefully remove pulp; cut into ¾-inch cubes. Wash and hull strawberries, reserving 4 to 6 whole berries for garnish. Cut strawberries in half. Chill all fruit. Just before serving, combine topping mixture, coconut, and fruit; spoon into cantaloupe shells; garnish with whole berries.

Lemonade

Makes 1 quart

½ cup sugar
½ cup lemon juice (2 lemons)
3 cups cold water

Add sugar to juice. Stir in cold water. Pour over ice in glasses. (Note: Roll lemons on table to make more juice.)

Tuna, Mushroom, and Tomato Quiche

Makes 6 servings

Pastry for 1 10-inch piecrust
4 eggs
1 tablespoon butter or margarine
¼ pound fresh mushrooms, sliced or 1 4-ounce can sliced mushrooms, drained
1 7-ounce can tuna in oil, drained
1 large tomato, peeled and sliced
1¾ cups milk
1 cup grated Swiss cheese
½ cup grated Gruyere cheese
¾ teaspoon salt
½ teaspoon paprika
¾ teaspoon grated onion

Preheat oven to 425°. Line a 10-inch quiche pan or pie plate with pastry, making sure that the crust is 2 inches higher than top of pan. Prick holes in the bottom of shell with fork; line bottom with foil. Place pastry weights on foil and bake 5 minutes. Remove weights and foil from shell; bake an additional 5 minutes. Cool; brush with 1 lightly beaten egg white; set aside. Reduce heat to 325°. If using fresh mushrooms melt butter in a skillet; add mushrooms; cook just until tender. Layer mushrooms, tuna, and tomato in pastry shell. Heat milk in a saucepan, add grated cheeses and stir until melted. Add salt, paprika, and onion. Remove from heat and beat in remaining 3 eggs and egg yolk one at a time. Pour mixture into pastry shell; bake for 45 minutes until custard is set.

Photo Opposite
CARROT QUICHE AND SUMMER BREEZE
from *Low Calorie Cookbook.* Copyright © 1981.
Published by Ideals Publishing Corp., Nashville, Tennessee.

Somebody's Mother

Mary Dow Brine

The woman was old and ragged and gray
And bent with the chill of the winter's day.

The street was wet with a recent snow
And the woman's feet were aged and slow.

She stood at the crossing and waited long,
Alone, uncared for, amid the throng

Of human beings who passed her by
Nor heeded the glance of her anxious eye.

Down the street, with laughter and shout,
Glad in the freedom of "school let out,"

Came the boys like a flock of sheep,
Hailing the snow piled white and deep.

Past the woman so old and gray
Hastened the children on their way.

Nor offered a helping hand to her—
So meek, so timid, afraid to stir

Lest the carriage wheels or the horse's feet
Should crowd her down in the slippery street.

At last came one of the merry troop,
The gayest laddie of all the group;

He paused beside her and whispered low,
"I'll help you cross, if you wish to go."

Her aged hand on his strong young arm
She placed, and so, without hurt or harm,

He guided the trembling feet along,
Proud that his own were firm and strong.

Then back again to his friends he went,
His young heart happy and well content.

"She's somebody's mother, boys, you know,
For all she's aged and poor and slow,

"And I hope some fellow will lend a hand
To help my mother, you understand,

"If ever she's poor and old and gray,
When her own dear boy is far away."

And "somebody's mother" bowed low her head
In her home that night, and the prayer she said

Was, "God be kind to the noble boy,
Who is somebody's son, and pride and joy!"

Photo Overleaf
ARCTIC POPPIES
ALASKA RANGE
Ed Cooper Photo

Mother's Day

Edgar A. Guest

Sons and daughters all over the country are wending their way home to be with Mother on Mother's Day. Millions won't be able to do this, but with the coming of that May Sunday dedicated and set apart to motherhood, they'll be writing to her, renewing their devotion and repeating, to her delight, the old tributes of affection. They'll be with her in spirit.

To those of us who have her now only in our memories the day will be one of rejoicing. If your heart is still torn with anguish; if the memory of her last day on earth is still fresh in your minds; if you are still in the shadow of her passing and conscious only of the great loss which you have suffered, you may not believe this, for it takes time. In a sense, which you shall some day come to experience, we are closer to our mothers now than ever before. She is with us now constantly. There are no partings; no long absences. We have only to think of her and she is with us. We can take her with us wherever we choose to go. We can wake, as children, in the night and her spirit hastens to be with us. Now she is never too ill to come, or too weary. In life the frequent absences were very real. Now neither time nor distance matter. Death has separated us only to bind us closer.

Gentle hands that ever weary toiling in love's
   vineyard sweet,
Eyes that seem forever cheery when our eyes
   they chance to meet,
Tender, patient, brave, devoted, this is always
   Mother's way.
Could her worth in gold be quoted as you think
   of her today?

There shall never be another quite so tender,
   quite so kind
As the patient little mother; nowhere on this
   earth you'll find
Her affection duplicated; none so proud if you
   are fine.
Could her worth be overstated? Not by any
   words of mine.

Death stood near the hour she bore us, agony
   was hers to know,
Yet she bravely faced it for us, smiling in her
   time of woe;
Down the years how oft we've tried her, often
   selfish, heedless, blind,
Yet with love alone to guide her she was never
   once unkind.

Vain are all our tributes to her if in words alone
   they dwell,
We must live the praises due her; there's no
   other way to tell
Gentle Mother that we love her. Would you
   say, as you recall
All the patient service of her, you've been
   worthy of it all?

John
Slobodnik

Hills in Spring

Beverly J. Anderson

I love to go out to the hills in spring
Where the skies are clear and blue,
Where caroling birds sing happily
And worldly cares seem few,
Where the apple orchards which I love
Bloom with blossoms fair,
Their fragrant perfume filling
The lovely springtime air.

I love to go out to the hills in spring
Where the woodland violets grow,
Where daisies white dot meadows green
And balmy breezes blow,
Where the children picking buttercups
Laugh and sing with glee,
Caressed by the sun's warm glow
As they play merrily.

I love to go out to the hills in spring
Where the world seems so serene,
Where silvery brooks murmur softly
And all is pleasant and green,
Where the view of the sun-kissed valley
Fills me with delight,
As nature's springtime splendor
Doth burst upon my sight.

I love to go out to the hills in spring
To rest 'neath the spacious sky,
And hear the song of the mockingbird
And watch the clouds drift by,
Where willowy trees sway to and fro
In the gentle breeze,
Where captured golden moments
Are treasured memories.

Photo Opposite
SUMMER DELIGHT
M. Thonig
H. Armstrong Roberts, Inc.

Now I Hear the Brook

Dorothy I. Neel

I used to hurry on my way,
So busy with each care-filled day
That in my haste to beat the clock,
I could not view a hollyhock,
Or watch the flight of zipping bees,
Nor care that brittle cold could freeze
The babbling of a brook.

Now I am forced to walk, not run.
With this new pace, I have begun
To savor all life's little things—
Sweet thrills when spring's first robin sings,
Quaint shyness in a pansy's face,
Soft healing warmth of rays which chase
The ice coat from a brook.

Thank God that now my steps are slow.
It took this change for me to know
In rushing, I had missed the best
Of life—those little things that rest
A weary soul that's worn from care.
In thankfulness, I breathe a prayer
For now I hear the brook.

Spring Song

Josepha Murray Emms

I sing of bright forsythia
That turns the earth to gold,
The gaiety of dogwood trees,
The beauty they unfold.

I sing of every rippling stream,
Radiant in the sun,
And skies of tender, smiling blue
Where angel clouds are spun.

I sing that winter now has fled
As voices greet my ear—
The croaking frogs awake the swamp
Proclaiming spring is here.

I join the chorus of the earth
In song to God on high,
Creator of this loveliness,
Whose name we glorify.

The Creek

Polly Byrd Taylor

Bounded by trees and bank,
I know my limitations,
My range of exploration,
My confines and my path.

I cannot change what's
In my path.
Rather than move
The obstacles,
I gently touch the
Boulders and
Continue.

I make my contribution
To the order of life.
My soft waters fashion
Small impressions in damp earth.
I feed the trees and fish
And insects. Children are happy
Splashing in me.

Never touching the same stone twice,
I move toward the ultimate,
Never knowing what is beyond,
But curious at my own pace,
Onward I flow.

Photo Opposite
BROOKSIDE BLOSSOMS
PELLA, WISCONSIN
Ken Dequaine

Summer Breeze

Joan Stephen

A summer breeze is lovely
As it gently moves the leaves—
Touching earth with softness,
Sweeping grass with ease.

A summer breeze is welcome
When the night is bright with stars—
Dancing with the moonbeams
To music from afar.

A summer breeze is cooling
As it moves in from the sea—
Playing in the sand dunes,
Embracing waves for free.

A summer breeze is poetry,
Speaking unknown words—
Whispering to daisies,
Praising hummingbirds.

A summer breeze is everywhere;
It crosses field and knoll—
The whole world loves the movement
As it wakens every soul.

Early Summer

Gertrude Dicks

In the time of early summer
When the earth's a bed of clover,
Every robin in my plum tree
Spills out joy in harmony.

Not a daisy on the hillside
Or wild berry by the wayside
Lacks the glory of the season
With its wonders just begun.

It's a time when hopes are highest
And the future looks the brightest,
And the rivers run refreshing,
Gurgling waters touching everything.

These are hours made for scheming
And a bit of happy dreaming,
For in early summer always
Comes the very best of days.

Summertime with *ideals*

"In the good old summertime..." is the wonderful feeling of the next issue, *Summertime Ideals*.

Imagine wandering lazily down a country lane bathed in sunbeams, inhaling deeply the aroma of meadowgrass heated by the midday sun, sensing the ripening of the earth in response to the kindess of the season.

And the kindness of people. Within the pages of *Summertime Ideals* you will find a celebration of family and friends through time—making new memories and sharing old ones.

Recently, Mr. Nicholas Percoco, of Staten Island, New York, wrote to say

As an artist, teacher, and nature enthusiast, I can assure you that your Ideals publication is a stroke of divine inspiration and a masterwork on paper to be treasured for years to come.

Thank you Mr. Percoco. We always enjoy hearing from readers and it is our sincere pleasure to provide issues which inspire and enrich each of you. And in the spirit of summertime, why not share a gift subscription with a friend, beginning with *Summertime Ideals*.

ACKNOWLEDGMENTS

SOMEBODY'S MOTHER by Mary Dow Brine from *THE BEST LOVED POEMS OF THE AMERICAN PEOPLE*, copyright 1936 by Garden City Publishing Co., Inc.; MOTHER'S DAY from *EDGAR A. GUEST BROADCASTING*, copyright 1935, The Reilly & Lee Co. Used by permission; MY FAVORITE RECIPES, A THOUSAND MILLION QUESTIONS, and JUST LIKE MINE from *POEMS FROM MY HEART*, copyright 1964 by Phyllis C. Michael, published by Zondervan Publishing House. Used by permission of the author; COMING OF MAY from *THORNS AND THISTLEDOWN* by Stella Craft Tremble, copyright 1954. Used by permission. Our sincere thanks to the following whose addresses we were unable to locate: Josephine Wiley Courtney for TO MOTHER; Lee Duncan Gray for A TREASURED GIFT; Blanche B. Landers for MY MOTHER'S CHILD; Reita Rea Simpson for BUTTONS; Ruth Rodier Taylor for TO MY SON.